A Comprehensive Look on Deism

Karl S. Moretti

Published by Dianoetic Publishing, 2023.

A COMPREHENSIVE LOOK ON DEISM

First edition. February 22, 2023.

Written by Karl S. Moretti.

Table of Contents

What is Deism and how does it differ from other religious beliefs?

Deism is a philosophical and theological belief system that emerged during the Enlightenment period in Europe and America, and which posits that the existence of God can be inferred from the natural world, without recourse to religious scripture or divine revelation. Deists believe in a single, supreme being, who created the universe and its natural laws, but who does not interfere in human affairs or reveal himself to humanity through miracles or religious texts.

Deism differs from many other religious beliefs in a number of ways. For example, Deism is characterized by a rejection of religious dogma, revelation, and ecclesiastical authority, instead placing emphasis on the use of reason and scientific observation to understand the nature of God and the universe. This stands in contrast to many traditional religions, which rely on sacred texts, religious authorities, and supernatural experiences to understand the divine.

Moreover, Deism is often associated with a more rationalistic and scientific approach to understanding the natural world and the divine, in which the laws of nature are seen as evidence of God's existence and power. This stands in contrast to more mystical and spiritual approaches to understanding the divine in which the focus is on personal religious experiences or direct communication with the divine.

Another important aspect of Deism is its emphasis on the natural and the rational, with an emphasis on the importance of human reason and understanding in making sense of the world. This stands in contrast to many religious beliefs that emphasize the importance of faith, revelation, and belief in the supernatural.

Finally, Deism has often been associated with political and social movements that emphasize individual freedom and equality, and a rejection of traditional authority and hierarchy. This stands in contrast to many traditional religious institutions which have often been seen as upholding conservative social and political values.

Overall, Deism is a complex and multifaceted belief system that differs from many other religious beliefs in its emphasis on reason, the natural world, and individual freedom and equality. It has played an important role in the history of Western thought and has continued to be influential in the development of modern secular and humanistic values.

Who were some of the most influential Deists in history?

Deism has had a rich history that spans several centuries and has been influential in shaping the philosophical, scientific, and political thought of many societies. As such, there have been many notable figures who have contributed to the development and spread of Deism throughout history. Here is a detailed account of some of the most influential Deists in history:

Thomas Paine: An English-born writer and political activist, Thomas Paine was one of the most influential Deists of the 18th century. Paine's writings, including his book "The Age of Reason," were instrumental in popularizing Deism in the United States and Europe, and helped to inspire the American Revolution.

Thomas Jefferson: An American Founding Father and the third President of the United States, Thomas Jefferson was a prominent Deist and was deeply influenced by the ideas of John Locke and other Enlightenment thinkers. Jefferson's commitment to religious freedom and separation of church and state was informed by his Deist beliefs.

Benjamin Franklin: Another prominent Founding Father, Benjamin Franklin was a Deist who played an important role in the development of science and technology in the 18th century. Franklin's experiments with electricity and his advocacy for scientific inquiry were grounded in his belief in the natural world and the power of reason.

Voltaire: A French Enlightenment writer and philosopher, Voltaire was a prominent Deist who championed the cause of reason, science, and tolerance. Voltaire's satirical works, such as "Candide," challenged religious dogma and helped to popularize Deist ideas throughout Europe.

David Hume: A Scottish philosopher and historian, David Hume was a key figure in the development of modern skepticism and empiricism. Hume's arguments against the existence of miracles and his emphasis on the importance of empirical evidence in understanding the natural world were influential in the development of Deist thought.

Baruch Spinoza: A Dutch philosopher of Sephardi Jewish origin, Baruch Spinoza was a radical thinker who challenged traditional religious beliefs and advocated for a rational and scientific approach to understanding the world. Spinoza's ideas about the unity of nature and the role of reason in understanding the divine were influential in the development of Deism.

Isaac Newton: An English mathematician and physicist, Isaac Newton was a devout Christian who nevertheless contributed to the development of Deist ideas through his scientific discoveries. Newton's laws of motion and theory of gravitation helped to explain the workings of the natural world, and provided evidence for the existence of a rational and orderly universe.

A COMPREHENSIVE LOOK ON DEISM

Ethan Allen: An American Revolutionary War hero and founder of the state of Vermont, Ethan Allen was a prominent Deist who championed the cause of religious freedom and individual rights. Allen's ideas about the importance of reason and the natural world were influential in the development of Deist thought in America.

John Toland: An Irish-born writer and philosopher, John Toland was a key figure in the development of Deist thought in the early 18th century. Toland's advocacy for a naturalistic approach to religion and his emphasis on the importance of reason and inquiry helped to lay the groundwork for the spread of Deism throughout Europe.

Paul Henri Thiry, Baron d'Holbach: A French philosopher and writer, Baron d'Holbach was a prominent Deist who advocated for a naturalistic approach to understanding the world. d'Holbach's works, such as "System of Nature," challenged traditional religious beliefs and emphasized the importance of scientific inquiry and rational thought.

These are just a few examples of the many influential Deists who have contributed to the development and spread of Deist thought throughout history. Through their advocacy for individual rights, religious freedom, and the importance of scientific inquiry, Deists have played a vital role in shaping the political and cultural landscape of many societies.

Deism has also had a significant impact on the development of other religious and philosophical movements, such as Unitarianism, Transcendentalism, and the Enlightenment. Deist ideas about the natural world, the importance of reason, and the rejection of religious dogma and superstition have been influential in shaping these movements and have helped to promote a more open and tolerant approach to religious and philosophical inquiry.

In addition to the figures listed above, there have been many other influential Deists throughout history, including Jean-Jacques Rousseau, James Madison, John Locke, and many others. Collectively, these figures have helped to promote a more rational and scientific approach to understanding the world and have contributed to the development of many of the social, cultural, and political movements that we take for granted today.

What were some of the key tenets of Deism during the Enlightenment period?

Deism emerged as a significant philosophical and religious movement during the Enlightenment period, which spanned the 17th and 18th centuries. During this time, Deists put forth a number of key tenets that distinguished their beliefs from other religious and philosophical traditions of the time. Here are some of the most important tenets of Deism during the Enlightenment period:

The existence of God: Deists believed in the existence of God, but rejected traditional religious dogma and superstition. They viewed God as a rational, benevolent, and all-knowing creator who had set the universe in motion, but who did not intervene in the affairs of human beings.

Reason and inquiry: Deists emphasized the importance of reason and inquiry in understanding the natural world and the divine. They believed that the universe operated according to natural laws and that these laws could be understood through scientific inquiry and the use of reason.

Natural theology: Deists believed that the natural world provided evidence for the existence of God. They argued that the complexity, order, and beauty of the universe demonstrated the existence of a rational and benevolent creator.

Religious toleration: Deists believed in the importance of religious toleration and the rejection of religious persecution. They argued that individuals should be free to pursue their own religious beliefs and that the state should not enforce any particular religion.

Separation of church and state: Deists advocated for the separation of church and state. They believed that religion should be a matter of individual conscience and that the state should not have the power to enforce any particular religious beliefs.

Individual rights: Deists believed in the importance of individual rights and freedoms. They argued that individuals had the right to pursue their own happiness and that the state should not infringe upon these rights.

Morality and ethics: Deists believed in the importance of morality and ethics, but rejected traditional religious morality based on divine revelation. They argued that morality was based on reason and that ethical principles could be derived from an understanding of natural law.

The importance of education: Deists believed in the importance of education and the cultivation of knowledge. They argued that individuals should be educated in the natural sciences, philosophy, and history in order to understand the world and the role of human beings within it.

A COMPREHENSIVE LOOK ON DEISM

Overall, Deists during the Enlightenment period put forth a vision of the universe and human society that emphasized reason, inquiry, toleration, and individual freedom. Their beliefs represented a rejection of traditional religious dogma and superstition and a commitment to a more rational and scientific approach to understanding the world. These ideas were influential in shaping the political and cultural landscape of many societies and helped to promote a more open and tolerant approach to religious and philosophical inquiry.

How did Deism influence the development of scientific thought in the 18th century?

Deism played a significant role in the development of scientific thought during the 18th century. Deists believed that the universe operated according to natural laws that could be understood through scientific inquiry and the use of reason. This belief had a profound impact on the way that many people thought about science and helped to lay the groundwork for the scientific revolution of the 17th and 18th centuries.

Deists rejected traditional religious explanations of natural phenomena and instead sought to explain the world through natural causes. They argued that the universe operated according to natural laws that could be understood through scientific inquiry and the use of reason. This approach to science helped to promote a more rational and empirical approach to understanding the natural world.

Deists also emphasized the importance of observation and experimentation in scientific inquiry. They argued that scientific theories should be based on empirical evidence and that scientists should be open to revising their theories in light of new evidence. This approach to science helped to promote a more open and collaborative approach to scientific inquiry and laid the groundwork for the development of the scientific method.

Deists were also influential in promoting scientific education and the cultivation of scientific knowledge. They believed that individuals should be educated in the natural sciences, philosophy, and history in order to understand the world and the role of human beings within it. This emphasis on education helped to promote a more informed and scientifically literate public and laid the groundwork for the development of modern scientific institutions.

In addition to their influence on scientific thought, Deists were also influential in promoting the development of technologies that would improve the human condition. They believed that science and technology could be used to promote human happiness and well-being and to alleviate suffering and hardship. This approach to science helped to promote a more utilitarian approach to technology and laid the groundwork for the development of modern technological innovations.

Overall, Deism played a significant role in the development of scientific thought during the 18th century. Their emphasis on reason, inquiry, and empirical evidence helped to promote a more rational and scientific approach to understanding the world and laid the groundwork for the development of modern scientific institutions and technologies.

How did Deists view the concept of God and the afterlife?

Deists viewed the concept of God and the afterlife in a unique way that set them apart from many other religious traditions. Deists believed that God was an impersonal and distant force that created the universe and established natural laws, but did not intervene in the affairs of humans. They believed that God was not concerned with human morality or individual lives, but rather with the overall balance and order of the universe.

In terms of the afterlife, Deists generally believed in a form of naturalistic immortality, where the soul would continue to exist after death, but without any kind of conscious awareness or individual identity. They believed that the soul was immortal because it was a part of the natural order of the universe, rather than because of any divine intervention or reward/punishment system.

Deists also rejected many traditional religious beliefs about the nature of God and the afterlife, including the idea of miracles, divine revelations, and the concept of a personal relationship with God. They believed that these beliefs were based on superstition and irrationality, rather than reason and evidence.

Deists also rejected many traditional religious practices and institutions, including the authority of the church, religious texts, and religious leaders. They believed that individuals should use reason and evidence to determine their beliefs about the world and the nature of God, rather than relying on religious authority.

Overall, Deists viewed the concept of God and the afterlife in a unique and non-traditional way that set them apart from many other religious traditions. They believed in a distant and impersonal God, and a form of naturalistic immortality that did not involve any kind of divine intervention or reward/punishment system. They rejected many traditional religious beliefs, practices, and institutions in favor of reason, evidence, and individual inquiry.

What is the relationship between Deism and natural theology?

D eism and natural theology are two related but distinct intellectual movements that emerged in the 17th and 18th
centuries. While there is some overlap between the two, there are
also important differences that set them apart.

Natural theology is a branch of theology that seeks to understand the nature of God and his attributes through the study
of the natural world. Natural theologians believe that the existence and attributes of God can be inferred from the natural order of the universe, which they see as evidence of God's handi-
work. Natural theologians use philosophical arguments and empirical evidence to make their case for the existence of God and
his attributes.

Deism, on the other hand, is a religious and philosophical movement that emphasizes the natural order of the universe and rejects traditional religious doctrines and supernatural beliefs. Deists believe in a distant and impersonal God who created the universe and established natural laws, but who does not intervene in the affairs of humans. Deists reject many traditional religious beliefs, practices, and institutions in favor of reason, evidence, and individual inquiry.

While Deism and natural theology are distinct movements, they share some common ground. Both emphasize the importance of reason and empirical evidence in understanding the natural world, and both seek to understand the nature of God through the study of the natural order of the universe. Natural theologians and Deists both reject many traditional religious beliefs, practices, and institutions in favor of a more rational and empirical approach to religion and theology.

However, there are also important differences between Deism and natural theology. Deists tend to be more skeptical of traditional religious beliefs and institutions, while natural theologians tend to see them as valuable sources of knowledge and guidance. Deists also tend to reject the idea of divine revelation, while natural theologians may see it as a legitimate source of knowledge about the nature of God.

In summary, Deism and natural theology are two related but distinct intellectual movements that emerged in the 17th and 18th centuries. While they share some common ground in their emphasis on reason and empirical evidence, they also have important differences that set them apart. Deism emphasizes the natural order of the universe and rejects traditional religious doctrines and supernatural beliefs, while natural theology seeks to understand the nature of God through the study of the natural world and may see traditional religious beliefs and institutions as valuable sources of knowledge and guidance.

How did Deists reconcile their belief in God with the problem of evil?

The problem of evil is one of the most enduring philosophical and theological problems, and Deists, like many other religious traditions, have grappled with this issue. The problem of evil refers to the question of how to reconcile the existence of evil and suffering in the world with the belief in an all-powerful and benevolent God.

Deists believed in a distant and impersonal God who created the universe and established natural laws, but who does not intervene in the affairs of humans. They believed that the natural order of the universe reflected the will of God, and that the existence of evil and suffering in the world was a result of human free will, rather than divine intervention.

One way that Deists reconciled their belief in God with the problem of evil was through the concept of moral responsibility. Deists believed that humans were free to make their own choices, and that they were responsible for the consequences of those choices. They believed that evil and suffering in the world were a result of human choices, rather than divine intervention, and that humans had the power to choose good over evil.

Deists also believed that the existence of evil and suffering in the world could serve a larger purpose, such as moral education or the testing of human character. They believed that overcoming adversity and suffering could lead to personal growth and moral development, and that this was an important part of the human experience.

Another way that Deists reconciled their belief in God with the problem of evil was through the concept of theodicy. Theodicy is the branch of theology that seeks to justify the existence of evil in the world in light of the belief in an all-powerful and benevolent God. Deists used philosophical arguments to defend their belief in God in the face of the problem of evil, arguing that God had created the world with a certain balance and order, and that this balance and order could not exist without the possibility of evil and suffering.

Overall, Deists reconciled their belief in God with the problem of evil by emphasizing human free will and moral responsibility, the larger purposes that evil and suffering could serve, and the philosophical arguments that defended the existence of God in the face of the problem of evil. While the problem of evil remains a difficult and complex issue, Deists sought to reconcile their belief in God with this problem in a way that emphasized reason, evidence, and personal responsibility.

How did Deists view the Bible and religious authority?

Deists held a unique perspective on the Bible and religious authority. While they acknowledged the importance of religious belief and the need for moral guidance, they also challenged traditional sources of religious authority and questioned the literal interpretation of religious texts.

Deists believed that the Bible was a human work, rather than a divine one, and that it was subject to historical and cultural influences that affected its interpretation. They rejected the idea of biblical inerrancy, and instead emphasized the importance of reason and rationality in interpreting religious texts. They believed that reason was a necessary tool for understanding God's will and that this understanding was open to all people, rather than being restricted to a select few.

Deists also challenged the authority of religious institutions, arguing that they often became corrupt and overly concerned with power and influence. They believed that religious institutions should be subject to reason and critical analysis, and that individuals should be free to worship in a way that reflected their own conscience and beliefs.

Despite their skepticism towards traditional sources of religious authority, Deists did not reject the importance of religious belief altogether. They believed that faith was an essential component of a moral and virtuous life, but that this faith should be grounded in reason and rational inquiry. They believed that the pursuit of truth and knowledge was a religious duty, and that individuals should be free to seek truth and meaning through their own intellectual and spiritual pursuits.

Overall, Deists held a complex and nuanced view of religious authority, recognizing the importance of religious belief and moral guidance, while also challenging traditional sources of religious authority and emphasizing the importance of reason and rationality in religious interpretation. They believed that faith and reason could coexist, and that a critical, open-minded approach to religious belief was essential for personal and moral growth.

Is there a deist perspective on the meaning of life?

Deism is a religious and philosophical movement that emerged in the Enlightenment era and emphasizes the use of reason and observation to understand the natural world and the human experience. While Deism is not a dogmatic or prescriptive religion, it does offer a perspective on the meaning of life that is informed by its central beliefs and principles.

One of the central beliefs of Deism is the idea that God, or a creative force, is present in the natural world, but does not intervene in human affairs. Deists believe that humans have the ability to reason and use their own experiences to understand the world around them. This emphasis on individual autonomy and the importance of reason and observation provides a basis for the Deist perspective on the meaning of life.

Deists believe that the purpose of life is to seek happiness and fulfillment through the use of reason, experience, and observation. They view the natural world as a source of wonder and inspiration, and believe that individuals should use their own powers of observation and reasoning to understand and appreciate it. This perspective emphasizes the importance of personal autonomy and the ability of individuals to make their own decisions about how to live their lives.

At the same time, Deists also believe that individuals have a responsibility to live in harmony with others and to promote the common good. They view the pursuit of individual happiness and fulfillment as part of a larger effort to create a just and harmonious society. This emphasis on the importance of social responsibility and cooperation provides a basis for the Deist perspective on ethics and morality.

In summary, the Deist perspective on the meaning of life emphasizes the importance of individual autonomy, reason, and observation in understanding and appreciating the natural world. It emphasizes the pursuit of happiness and fulfillment as part of a larger effort to create a just and harmonious society, and stresses the importance of social responsibility and cooperation in achieving this goal. While Deism does not offer a dogmatic or prescriptive view of the meaning of life, its

principles and beliefs provide a framework for individuals to develop their own perspective on this fundamental question.

What was the impact of Deism on religious tolerance and pluralism?

Deism had a significant impact on religious tolerance and pluralism, particularly during the Enlightenment period. Deists rejected many of the dogmatic and exclusive beliefs of traditional Christianity and sought to promote a more open and inclusive approach to religious belief.

One of the key principles of Deism was the idea that reason and rational inquiry were essential for understanding God's will. This belief led many Deists to reject the strict dogmatism of traditional Christianity and to promote a more tolerant and inclusive approach to religious belief. They argued that people of different faiths could come to a common understanding of the divine through the use of reason and critical analysis, rather than through blind adherence to religious authority.

Deists also rejected the idea of religious persecution, arguing that it was contrary to the principles of reason and morality. They believed that individuals should be free to practice their own religion without fear of persecution or discrimination. This belief in religious freedom and tolerance was a significant departure from the intolerance and persecution that had characterized much of Europe's religious history.

The influence of Deism on religious tolerance and pluralism can be seen in many historical developments. For example, the United States Constitution, which was heavily influenced by Enlightenment principles, includes provisions for religious freedom and the separation of church and state. These principles were rooted in the Enlightenment belief in reason and tolerance, and reflected a rejection of the dogmatism and intolerance of traditional Christianity.

In addition, Deism played a significant role in the development of religious pluralism in Europe and America. The emphasis on reason and critical inquiry allowed individuals to explore and question their own beliefs, and to come to their own understanding of the divine. This led to a diverse array of religious beliefs and practices, and contributed to the growth of religious pluralism in many parts of the world.

Overall, Deism had a profound impact on religious tolerance and pluralism, promoting a more open and inclusive approach to religious belief that valued reason and critical inquiry over dogmatism and intolerance. Its influence can be seen in many historical developments, including the growth of religious freedom, the separation of church and state, and the development of religious pluralism in many parts of the world.

What is the relationship between Deism and the concept of the divine right of kings?

Deism emerged as a religious and philosophical movement in the Enlightenment era, which challenged traditional religious dogma and authority. One of the most significant aspects of this challenge was the questioning of the divine right of kings, which had been a central political and religious concept for centuries. The divine right of kings was the belief that monarchs derived their authority to rule directly from God, and that their power was therefore absolute and unquestionable.

Deists rejected this idea of divine right, arguing that individuals had inherent rights and freedoms that were not granted by any divine authority or monarch. They believed that individuals had the right to govern themselves, rather than being subject to the arbitrary and unjust rule of a monarch. This rejection of divine right was based on the Deist belief in the rationality and autonomy of the individual, as well as their rejection of religious dogma and the authority of religious institutions.

Deists also believed that the authority to govern should be based on the consent of the governed, rather than the divine right of a monarch. They argued that governments should be established to protect individual rights and promote the common good, rather than being used to serve the interests of a particular ruler or ruling class. This idea of popular sovereignty and government by consent laid the foundation for the development of modern democratic theory and practice.

The rejection of the divine right of kings by Deists also had important implications for the relationship between religion and politics. Deists believed that the role of religion was to promote moral and ethical values, rather than to provide a basis for political authority. They argued that individuals had the right to interpret religious and moral principles for themselves, rather than relying on the authority of religious institutions or figures. This emphasis on individual reason and conscience helped to establish the separation of church and state, which became a central principle of modern democratic theory.

In summary, Deism had a significant impact on the concept of the divine right of kings. Deists rejected the idea that monarchs derived their authority directly from God and argued that individuals had inherent rights and freedoms that should not be subject to the arbitrary and unjust rule of a monarch. They emphasized the importance of popular sovereignty and government by consent, and helped to establish the separation of church and state as a fundamental principle of modern democratic theory.

How did Deists view the relationship between reason and faith?

Deists viewed the relationship between reason and faith in a distinct and novel way that differed from the prevailing views of their time. During the Enlightenment, Deists sought to reconcile the discoveries of science and the use of reason with their beliefs about God and the universe. They believed that the use of reason was essential for understanding God and the natural world, and that faith should be based on rational inquiry and evidence, rather than dogma and blind acceptance.

In the Deist view, reason and faith were not opposed to each other, but rather were complementary. Deists believed that reason and evidence should inform faith and religious beliefs, and that faith should not be based on arbitrary claims or unprovable assertions. Instead, Deists believed that the study of nature and reason could lead to a better understanding of God and the natural world, and that faith should be based on a rational inquiry into the evidence.

Deists also rejected the idea that faith required the suspension of reason or the acceptance of claims that were contrary to evidence. They believed that faith should be based on a careful examination of the evidence and that religious beliefs should be subject to the same standards of reason and evidence as other areas of inquiry.

The emphasis on reason and evidence in Deism led to a rejection of many traditional religious beliefs that were seen as unsupported by evidence or irrational. Deists rejected the idea of miracles, arguing that the laws of nature were fixed and unchanging and that God did not intervene in the natural world. They also rejected the idea of divine revelation, arguing that the only source of knowledge about God was reason and the study of nature.

Deists viewed reason and evidence as the foundation for faith and religious beliefs, and this emphasis on reason had a profound influence on the development of religious thought in the Enlightenment period. The Deist approach to the relationship between reason and faith helped to establish a more critical and rational approach to religious inquiry, which had a significant impact on the development of religious and philosophical thought in the centuries that followed.

What is the relationship between Deism and humanism?

Deism and humanism share a number of fundamental beliefs, which have led to close connections between the two philosophies. Both Deism and humanism emerged during the Enlightenment period, which was marked by a strong emphasis on reason, individualism, and the pursuit of knowledge. These shared values have led to a natural affinity between Deism and humanism, as both philosophies seek to promote rational inquiry, critical thinking, and the elevation of human dignity and worth.

At its core, Deism is a philosophy that stresses the importance of reason and evidence in understanding God and the universe. Deists reject many of the traditional religious dogmas and practices that they view as unsupported by reason or evidence. Instead, they believe that the study of nature and reason can lead to a better understanding of God and the natural world. Deism also emphasizes the importance of individual conscience and free will, as well as the inherent dignity and worth of each person.

Humanism, in turn, is a philosophy that emphasizes the value and agency of human beings, individually and collectively. Humanism also emphasizes the importance of reason, evidence, and critical thinking in the pursuit of knowledge and the promotion of ethical behavior. Humanists value individual freedom, human rights, and human dignity, and they often focus on the development of human potential and the improvement of human society.

There are a number of areas where Deism and humanism intersect. For example, both philosophies value reason and evidence as essential tools for understanding the world and shaping ethical behavior. Both also emphasize the importance of individual conscience and free will, and the inherent worth and dignity of each human being. In addition, both Deism and humanism reject dogmatic religious claims and promote a more critical, rational approach to understanding God and the natural world.

The Deist focus on reason and evidence has also led to a strong emphasis on individual freedom and autonomy, which is a key element of humanist thought. Humanists often emphasize the importance of personal autonomy and self-determination, and they reject the idea of blindly accepting authority or tradition without question. This focus on individual autonomy and freedom is a key aspect of Deism as well.

A COMPREHENSIVE LOOK ON DEISM

In summary, Deism and humanism share a number of fundamental beliefs and values, including an emphasis on reason and evidence, individual freedom and autonomy, and the inherent dignity and worth of each human being. The close connections between these two philosophies reflect a common commitment to the pursuit of knowledge, critical thinking, and ethical behavior, and have contributed to the development of both religious and secular thought in the centuries since the Enlightenment.

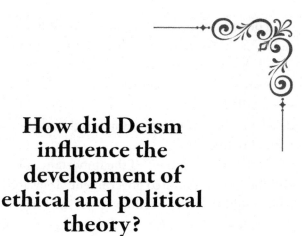

How did Deism influence the development of ethical and political theory?

Deism, a philosophical and religious movement that emerged in the Enlightenment era, had a significant influence on the development of ethical and political theory. Deists believed in a rational and moral system of thought that relied on individual reason and conscience, rather than religious dogma or tradition. As such, Deist ideas contributed to the development of new ethical and political theories that focused on individual rights, liberty, and equality.

One of the primary ways that Deism influenced ethical and political theory was through its rejection of traditional religious dogma and authority. Deists believed that individuals had the right to interpret religious and moral principles for themselves, rather than relying on the authority of religious institutions or figures. This emphasis on individual reason and conscience had significant implications for the development of ethical and political theory.

For example, Deists argued that individuals had inherent rights, such as the right to life, liberty, and property. They believed that these rights were not granted by a divine authority, but were instead inherent to human beings by virtue of their existence. This idea of inherent rights laid the foundation for the development of modern human rights theory and the idea of natural rights.

Deists also emphasized the importance of individual liberty and the need for limited government. They argued that individuals should have the freedom to pursue their own interests and beliefs, without interference from the government or other external authorities. This idea of individual liberty laid the foundation for the development of liberal political theory, which emphasizes the importance of individual rights and freedom.

In addition, Deists were often critical of authoritarian governments and social structures. They believed that individuals should have equal opportunities to pursue their own interests and achieve success, regardless of their social or economic status. This idea of social and economic equality laid the foundation for the development of modern political and economic theories that emphasize the importance of social justice and equality.

Moreover, Deists argued that individuals had a responsibility to use their reason and conscience to make ethical and moral decisions. They rejected the idea of blind faith and emphasized the importance of critical thinking and rational analysis in making ethical and moral judgments. This idea of individual responsibility and critical thinking laid the foundation for the development of modern ethical theories, such as consequentialism and deontological ethics.

A COMPREHENSIVE LOOK ON DEISM

In summary, Deism had a significant influence on the development of ethical and political theory. Deist ideas challenged traditional religious dogma and authority, emphasized the importance of individual reason and conscience, and laid the foundation for the development of modern ethical and political theories that focused on individual rights, liberty, and equality. Deism helped to establish a new moral and ethical framework that relied on reason, critical thinking, and individual responsibility, rather than religious tradition or dogma.

How did Deism influence the development of Romanticism in literature and the arts?

Deism played a significant role in the development of Romanticism, a cultural and artistic movement that emerged in the late 18th century and flourished in the 19th century. Romanticism was characterized by a strong emphasis on emotion, individualism, and the imagination, as well as a fascination with the natural world and a rejection of the strict rules and conventions of the Enlightenment era.

One of the key ways that Deism influenced Romanticism was through its emphasis on the natural world and the divine order of the universe. Deists believed that God created the world and established its laws, but that the universe was self-regulating and governed by natural processes. This view of the world as a self-regulating system inspired Romantic artists and writers to explore the beauty and complexity of the natural world, and to celebrate its majesty and power.

Deism also influenced Romanticism by encouraging a more individualistic and emotional approach to spirituality and morality. Deists believed that individuals were capable of understanding God's will through reason and conscience, rather than through dogmatic religious authorities or traditions. This emphasis on individualism and the inner self inspired Romantic writers and artists to explore their own emotions, desires, and experiences, and to create works that expressed their personal visions and perspectives.

Another way that Deism influenced Romanticism was through its emphasis on the power of the imagination. Deists believed that the human mind was capable of understanding the divine order of the universe, and that this understanding could be achieved through reason and imagination. This emphasis on the imagination inspired Romantic writers and artists to create works that were highly imaginative and fantastic, and that explored the depths of the human psyche and the mysteries of the universe.

Overall, Deism played a significant role in the development of Romanticism, through its emphasis on the natural world, individualism, and the imagination. Deist ideas encouraged artists and writers to explore their own emotions, desires, and experiences, and to create works that expressed their personal visions and perspectives. This approach to creativity and spirituality had a lasting impact on the arts and literature of the 19th century, and contributed to the development of the modernist and postmodernist movements in the 20th century.

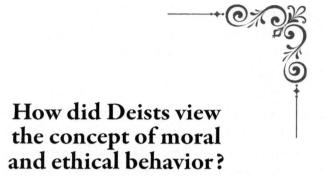

How did Deists view the concept of moral and ethical behavior?

Deists believed in the importance of moral and ethical behavior, but they approached these concepts from a rational and individualistic perspective. They believed that individuals were capable of understanding God's will through reason and conscience, rather than through dogmatic religious authorities or traditions.

Deists believed that ethical behavior was not a matter of following a set of rules or commandments, but rather a matter of using reason to understand the natural laws and order of the universe, and acting in accordance with this understanding. They believed that God had created the universe and established its laws, and that human beings could understand and follow these laws through the use of reason and conscience.

Deists also believed that ethical behavior was not limited to religious or spiritual matters, but extended to all areas of human life. They believed that individuals had a duty to act in accordance with the natural laws and principles that governed the universe, and that this required them to act with honesty, integrity, and compassion in their personal and professional lives.

Deists viewed morality and ethics as universal principles that applied to all human beings, regardless of their religious or cultural backgrounds. They believed that these principles were grounded in reason and nature, rather than in religious dogma or tradition, and that they could be discovered and understood through careful observation and reflection.

Overall, Deists viewed the concept of moral and ethical behavior as an essential part of human life, grounded in reason and conscience rather than in religious dogma or tradition. They believed that individuals were capable of understanding and following the natural laws and order of the universe, and that this required them to act with honesty, integrity, and compassion in all aspects of their lives.

What was the relationship between Deism and the development of science fiction?

The relationship between Deism and the development of science fiction is a complex one that has been the subject of much debate and analysis over the years. At its core, science fiction is a genre that explores the intersection of science and technology with human experience, often projecting these developments into imagined futures or alternate realities. Deism, with its emphasis on reason, natural law, and the pursuit of knowledge, provides a philosophical framework that is well-suited to the exploration of scientific and technological concepts.

Many of the key ideas and themes that are common in science fiction can be traced back to the Deist worldview. For example, the idea that the universe is governed by natural laws and principles that can be discovered and understood through reason is a key tenet of Deism. This concept is central to many science fiction stories, which often explore the implications of scientific and technological advancements within the framework of a rational and orderly universe.

In addition, Deism's rejection of traditional religious dogma and emphasis on individualism and rationality can be seen as an important influence on the development of science fiction as a genre. Science fiction often features protagonists who are outsiders, rebels, or scientists who challenge established systems of authority and tradition in pursuit of scientific truth and discovery. This focus on the individual as a force for change and progress can be seen as an extension of the Deist emphasis on individual freedom and autonomy.

Furthermore, Deism's emphasis on the pursuit of knowledge and scientific discovery can be seen as an important precursor to the scientific and technological themes that are common in science fiction. Many science fiction stories feature advanced technologies, alien civilizations, and alternate realities that are grounded in scientific principles and concepts. This fascination with science and technology as a means of unlocking the mysteries of the universe can be seen as an extension of the Deist emphasis on the pursuit of knowledge and understanding.

Overall, the relationship between Deism and the development of science fiction is a complex and multifaceted one. While it is difficult to pinpoint specific Deist influences on the genre, it is clear that many of the key ideas and themes that are common in science fiction can be traced back to the Deist worldview. The emphasis on reason, natural law, individualism, and the pursuit of knowledge that is central to Deism has provided a philosophical foundation that has allowed science fiction to explore the intersections of science, technology, and human experience in exciting and imaginative ways.

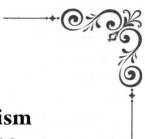

How did Deism influence the development of freethought and skepticism?

Deism was an important influence on the development of freethought and skepticism, particularly during the Enlightenment period. Freethought is a philosophical stance that holds that beliefs should be formed on the basis of reason, independent of tradition, authority, or established dogma. Skepticism, on the other hand, is a critical attitude that questions the validity of knowledge and beliefs, particularly those that are based on faith or supernatural claims.

Deism, with its emphasis on reason, natural law, and the pursuit of knowledge, provided a philosophical foundation that was well-suited to the development of freethought and skepticism. Many Deists were critical of established religious institutions and dogma, and sought to develop a more rational and empirical approach to understanding the world. This skepticism of traditional religious beliefs and authority was a key influence on the development of freethought and skepticism, particularly in the 18th and 19th centuries.

One of the most significant ways in which Deism influenced the development of freethought and skepticism was through its rejection of revealed religion. Deists rejected the idea that religious truths could be revealed through divine revelation, and instead emphasized the importance of reason and the pursuit of knowledge. This rejection of revealed religion was an important influence on the development of skepticism, as it led many thinkers to question the validity of religious claims that were based on faith rather than reason.

In addition, Deism's emphasis on individualism and personal freedom was an important influence on the development of freethought and skepticism. Many Deists believed that individuals should be free to pursue their own beliefs and ideas, and that traditional religious authorities should not be able to impose their beliefs on others. This emphasis on individualism and freedom provided a philosophical foundation that was well-suited to the development of freethought and skepticism, as it encouraged individuals to question established beliefs and authority.

Overall, the influence of Deism on the development of freethought and skepticism was significant, particularly during the Enlightenment period. The emphasis on reason, natural law, and the pursuit of knowledge provided a philosophical foundation that was well-suited to the development of freethought and skepticism, and the rejection of revealed religion and emphasis on individualism and personal freedom were important influences on the development of these philosophical stances.

How did Deists view the relationship between religion and politics?

Deists generally viewed the relationship between religion and politics as one that should be kept separate. This belief was based on the idea that the primary purpose of government was to protect individual rights and promote the general welfare, while the primary purpose of religion was to provide a framework for understanding the nature of the universe and our place in it. Deists believed that mixing religion and politics could lead to conflicts of interest and undermine the ability of government to serve the public good.

One of the key reasons for this belief was the historical experience of religious conflict and persecution. Deists recognized the dangers of allowing religious institutions to wield political power, as history had shown that religious institutions could be used to justify persecution, war, and other forms of oppression. Instead, Deists believed that government should be based on reason and natural law, and that religion should be a matter of personal belief and conscience.

Another factor that influenced the Deist view of the relationship between religion and politics was their belief in the importance of individual freedom and autonomy. Deists believed that individuals should be free to pursue their own beliefs and ideas, and that government should not interfere in matters of personal conscience. This view was based on the idea that individuals have the right to pursue their own happiness and fulfillment, and that government should be limited to protecting these rights rather than promoting specific religious beliefs.

Overall, the Deist view of the relationship between religion and politics was one that emphasized the importance of reason, individualism, and the separation of church and state. Deists recognized the dangers of allowing religious institutions to wield political power, and believed that government should be based on reason and natural law rather than religious authority. This view has had a significant impact on the development of political thought and institutions, and continues to be an important influence on modern political discourse.

What is the relationship between Deism and the concept of a "watchmaker God"?

The concept of a "watchmaker God" is a key component of Deist theology. This idea suggests that God is like a watchmaker who creates a complex machine (the universe) and sets it in motion, but then does not intervene in its ongoing operation. The watchmaker God is not involved in the day-to-day workings of the universe, but rather sets the laws of nature in motion and allows them to play out without interference.

The idea of a watchmaker God has its roots in the Enlightenment era, when many thinkers sought to reconcile their belief in God with their growing understanding of the natural world. Deists believed that God had created the universe and set its laws in motion, but that He did not intervene in its ongoing operation. This view was influenced by the scientific discoveries of the time, which showed that the universe operated according to natural laws that could be studied and understood through observation and experimentation.

The watchmaker God idea was also influenced by the philosophy of natural theology, which sought to understand the nature of God by studying the natural world. Natural theologians believed that the order and complexity of the universe provided evidence of God's existence and attributes, and the watchmaker God concept fit well with this approach. The idea was also compatible with the Deist belief in the importance of reason and natural law, as it suggested that God had created a rational and orderly universe that could be understood through observation and reason.

Despite its popularity among Deists, the watchmaker God idea was also criticized by some thinkers who argued that it was inconsistent with traditional religious beliefs. Critics argued that a God who did not intervene in the universe was not an active and involved God, and that the watchmaker concept reduced God to a mere engineer rather than a loving and compassionate creator. However, the idea of a watchmaker God continued to be influential in Deist thought and has had a lasting impact on the way many people view the relationship between God and the natural world.

How did Deism view the relationship between nature and God?

Deism views the relationship between nature and God as a harmonious one. According to Deist philosophy, God created the natural world and set it in motion with laws that govern its operation. However, God does not intervene in the natural world, allowing it to operate according to these laws. Deists believe that God is distant from the world and does not actively participate in the events that take place within it.

In this view, the natural world is seen as evidence of God's existence and power, but also as a self-sufficient and self-regulating system. Deists believe that the natural world operates according to fixed, immutable laws, and that these laws can be discovered and understood through observation and reason. This belief in the harmony of nature and God was central to Deist thought, as it emphasized the importance of reason, science, and natural law in understanding the world.

Deists also believed that the natural world was a reflection of God's goodness, wisdom, and power. They saw the natural world as evidence of God's perfection, and believed that the order and beauty of nature was a reflection of his divine nature. However, they also acknowledged that nature could be harsh and unforgiving, with disasters and disease often affecting people indiscriminately. In this view, Deists saw the natural world as a mixed blessing, with both beauty and danger.

Overall, Deism views the relationship between nature and God as one of mutual respect and harmony. While God is seen as the creator of the natural world, he is not seen as an active participant in its day-to-day operations, allowing the laws of nature to govern the world. This view emphasizes the importance of observation, reason, and science in understanding the natural world, while also acknowledging the beauty and power of nature as evidence of God's existence.

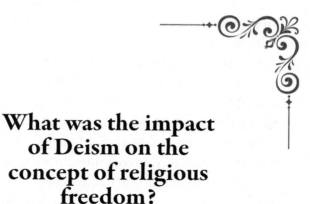

What was the impact of Deism on the concept of religious freedom?

Deism played a significant role in shaping the concept of religious freedom, particularly during the Enlightenment period. Deists believed that individuals had the right to follow their own path to God and that religious beliefs should be based on reason and rationality rather than dogma or tradition. As a result, Deists were often strong proponents of religious toleration and freedom of conscience.

In the 18th century, many European countries were still dominated by established churches that enjoyed special privileges and often persecuted dissidents. In England, for example, the Church of England was the official state religion and nonconformists, such as Baptists and Quakers, were subjected to various forms of discrimination. Deists, including influential figures such as Thomas Paine and Voltaire, were vocal critics of such religious intolerance and worked to promote the idea that religious freedom was a basic human right.

In the United States, which was founded in part on Enlightenment principles, Deism also played an important role in the development of religious freedom. Many of the Founding Fathers, including Thomas Jefferson and Benjamin Franklin, were influenced by Deist ideas and advocated for the separation of church and state. The First Amendment to the United States Constitution, which guarantees the freedom of religion, is often seen as a reflection of this commitment to religious toleration and the protection of individual conscience.

Deism also had an impact on the development of modern religious pluralism, which holds that multiple religions and spiritual traditions can coexist peacefully and even complement one another. By emphasizing the importance of reason and personal inquiry in religious belief, Deism paved the way for a more open and accepting attitude towards different faiths and worldviews. This legacy can be seen in the growth of interfaith dialogue and the increasing recognition of the value of diversity in religious and cultural life.

Overall, Deism's emphasis on individual conscience and the importance of reason and rationality in religious belief helped to promote the development of religious freedom and pluralism, both of which are now widely regarded as essential components of a just and democratic society.

How did Deists view the relationship between reason and revelation?

Deism is a religious and philosophical belief system that emphasizes the role of reason and observation in understanding the natural world and the existence of God. One of the key characteristics of Deism is the belief that God created the universe but does not intervene in it or in human affairs, and that the only way to learn about God is through the study of nature and reason, rather than through revelation or divine texts. As such, Deists generally view reason as a more reliable guide to truth than revelation, which they see as a source of superstition and dogmatism.

The relationship between reason and revelation in Deism can be understood in terms of the Deist rejection of supernaturalism. Deists reject the idea that the universe is governed by supernatural forces or that there are supernatural beings that intervene in human affairs. They believe that the laws of nature operate independently of any supernatural intervention, and that these laws can be discovered through reason and observation. In this sense, Deism is similar to naturalism and rationalism, which also emphasize the role of reason and natural phenomena in understanding the world.

Deists also reject the idea that divine revelation is necessary for human salvation or for understanding the nature of God. They believe that God has revealed himself through the natural world and that reason and observation are sufficient for discovering the truth about God's existence and attributes. This means that Deists do not rely on religious texts or authorities to interpret the nature of God or the universe, but instead rely on their own faculties of reason and observation.

In summary, the relationship between reason and revelation in Deism is one in which reason is seen as the primary means for understanding the universe and the existence of God. Deists reject supernaturalism and view the laws of nature as operating independently of any divine intervention. They also reject the idea that divine revelation is necessary for understanding God or for human salvation, and instead rely on reason and observation to discover the truth about the natural world and the nature of God.

What was the relationship between Deism and the concept of social justice?

Deism had a complex relationship with the concept of social justice. On one hand, Deism emphasized reason and natural law, and many Deists believed that individuals were responsible for creating a just society through the use of reason and the application of natural law. Deists believed that reason, rather than revelation or tradition, was the best guide for determining what actions were just and ethical. As such, many Deists were critical of social structures and practices that were based on tradition or custom, which they believed were often irrational or unjust.

On the other hand, some Deists were skeptical of the idea of social justice as a specific, defined concept. They believed that the natural order of things was determined by the laws of nature and that attempts to impose a particular social order or to redress social inequalities would be futile or even harmful. In this view, the best course of action was to allow society to evolve according to its natural tendencies and to promote individual freedom and self-reliance.

Overall, however, Deists played an important role in the development of the concept of social justice by emphasizing reason and the idea that individuals were responsible for creating a just society. Many Deists were also involved in political and social reform movements, such as the abolition of slavery, and they advocated for a more egalitarian society. Their belief in the equality of all individuals before God and their emphasis on reason and natural law helped to lay the groundwork for later social justice movements.

How did Deists view the concept of original sin and human nature?

Deists typically reject the doctrine of original sin, which posits that humans are inherently sinful and guilty due to the disobedience of Adam and Eve in the Garden of Eden. Rather, they tend to view humans as inherently good and capable of reason and virtue. In this sense, Deists are often optimistic about human nature and see individuals as having the potential to improve themselves and their societies through the use of reason.

The rejection of the concept of original sin is often linked to the Deistic emphasis on natural law and the belief that humans can discover moral truths through the exercise of reason and observation of the natural world. For Deists, moral behavior is not a matter of following divine commands or adhering to revealed religious texts, but rather is grounded in the laws of nature and reason.

Deists also tend to reject the idea of salvation or redemption through faith in a divine savior, which is often associated with the concept of original sin. Rather, they often view salvation as a matter of living a moral and virtuous life based on reason and natural law.

In summary, Deists generally view human nature as inherently good and capable of reason and virtue, and reject the concept of original sin and the associated doctrines of salvation and redemption through faith. They emphasize the importance of living a moral and virtuous life based on reason and natural law, rather than adhering to religious commandments or dogma.

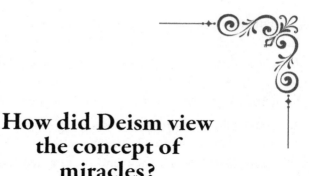

How did Deism view the concept of miracles?

Deism takes a rather skeptical view on the concept of miracles. Deists believe in a rational, naturalistic worldview, and the idea of supernatural intervention in the natural world is often seen as implausible or even impossible. The idea of a universe governed by natural laws means that the miraculous is generally not considered a valid explanation for events or phenomena that seem extraordinary or inexplicable.

Deists often reject the idea of miracles as a violation of the laws of nature, which are viewed as the product of a rational, intelligent creator rather than the capricious whims of a divine being. They argue that miracles cannot be proven, and that claims of miraculous events are often based on superstition, ignorance, or deceit. Instead, Deists tend to emphasize reason, evidence, and critical thinking as the best means of understanding the world and uncovering its mysteries.

Furthermore, Deists often view miracles as unnecessary for belief in God, as they see the natural world as a sufficient manifestation of the divine. The order and beauty of the universe, as well as the complexity and intelligence of living beings, are seen as evidence of a purposeful creator rather than the product of random chance or blind processes.

In conclusion, while Deists may acknowledge the possibility of extraordinary events, they tend to approach claims of miracles with skepticism and seek rational, naturalistic explanations for phenomena that may appear miraculous. The concept of a rational, intelligent universe governed by natural laws is central to Deist beliefs, and the idea of supernatural intervention is often viewed as incompatible with this worldview.

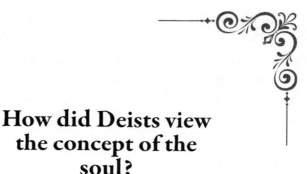

How did Deists view the concept of the soul?

Deism is a religious philosophy that emphasizes the natural order of the universe and rejects the idea of divine intervention in human affairs. As such, Deists typically view the concept of the soul as a matter of personal belief, rather than an objective truth.

Some Deists may believe in the existence of a soul or spirit, while others may reject the concept as a vestige of superstition. Generally, Deists see human beings as rational and autonomous individuals capable of living moral and ethical lives without the need for divine intervention.

In some cases, Deists may view the soul as an essential aspect of human nature that is distinct from the physical body. However, they generally reject the notion of an afterlife or eternal reward or punishment for the soul.

In the absence of divine revelation or authoritative religious texts, Deists tend to rely on reason, observation, and personal experience in their beliefs about the nature of the world and the human condition. As such, there is no single Deist view of the soul, and individual Deists may have differing opinions on this topic.

How did Deism influence the development of the concept of self-realization?

Deism influenced the development of the concept of self-realization in a number of ways, particularly in the context of the Enlightenment period. The Enlightenment was a time of intellectual and cultural change, and Deism played a significant role in this process. Deists rejected many of the traditional religious beliefs and practices of their time, and they sought to develop a more rational and naturalistic approach to understanding the world and the human experience.

One of the key tenets of Deism was the belief in the natural goodness of humanity. Deists believed that human beings were capable of understanding and experiencing the divine in their own lives, without the need for intermediaries such as priests or religious texts. This idea of individual agency and self-realization was a radical departure from traditional religious beliefs, which emphasized the need for obedience and submission to religious authority.

Deists also believed in the importance of reason and empirical observation in understanding the world. They rejected many of the supernatural claims made by traditional religions, such as miracles and divine intervention in the natural world. Instead, they saw the universe as a self-regulating, self-sustaining system that could be understood through reason and observation.

These ideas had a significant impact on the development of the concept of self-realization, which emphasizes the importance of individual agency, self-awareness, and self-determination in the pursuit of personal fulfillment and spiritual growth. By rejecting the idea of a transcendent, intervening God, Deists encouraged individuals to look within themselves for answers to life's big questions.

What was the relationship between Deism and the development of the concept of the individual conscience?

Deism was a philosophical and religious movement that emerged in the Enlightenment era and gained popularity in Europe and North America during the 17th and 18th centuries. Deists believed in the existence of a God who created the universe and established natural laws but did not intervene in the affairs of human beings. They rejected traditional religious dogma, supernatural events, and organized religions, instead, emphasizing the use of reason, observation, and personal experience to understand the world.

The deist view of God and the universe had a significant impact on the development of the concept of the individual conscience. Deists believed that each person had a direct and personal relationship with God, and that it was the responsibility of individuals to use their reason and conscience to understand and follow the natural laws established by God. This meant that individuals had the

freedom to interpret religious and moral principles for themselves, rather than relying on the authority of religious institutions or traditions.

Deists also believed that humans were capable of discovering moral truths through reason and experience, rather than solely through revelation or religious authority. This emphasis on individual reason and conscience contributed to the development of modern ethical and moral philosophy, including the ideas of natural rights, individual autonomy, and the social contract.

The deist concept of the individual conscience also influenced the development of religious freedom and toleration. Deists believed that individuals should be free to worship or not worship as they chose, and that religious beliefs and practices should not be enforced by the state or imposed on others. This emphasis on individual freedom and choice was a precursor to modern ideas of religious pluralism and the separation of church and state.

A COMPREHENSIVE LOOK ON DEISM

In summary, the deist movement, with its emphasis on reason, personal experience, and individual conscience, played a significant role in the development of modern ethical and moral philosophy, religious freedom and toleration, and individual autonomy. The deist view of God and the universe challenged traditional religious authority and paved the way for a more secular and rational approach to understanding the world and our place in it.

How did Deism influence the development of the concept of human rights?

Deism was a philosophical and religious movement that emerged in the Enlightenment era, which emphasized the use of reason and observation to understand the world and challenged traditional religious authority. Deists believed in the existence of a God who created the universe and established natural laws but did not intervene in the affairs of human beings. They rejected supernatural events, organized religion, and dogmatic beliefs, instead emphasizing individual reason and conscience to interpret religious and moral principles.

The deist view of God and the universe had a significant impact on the development of the concept of human rights. Deists believed that individuals had natural rights, such as the right to life, liberty, and property, that were inherent and not granted by any authority, including the state. They saw these rights as being based on natural law, which could be discovered through reason and observation, rather than being dependent on religious revelation or traditional authority.

Deists also believed in the equality of all people, regardless of social status, race, or religion. This belief was influenced by the idea that God created all humans, and thus, all individuals were equally valuable in the eyes of God. Deists rejected the idea that some people were born with special privileges or rights, such as those associated with aristocracy or monarchy, and instead argued that all people were entitled to the same rights and protections.

The deist view of natural rights and equality was influential in the development of modern human rights. The Universal Declaration of Human Rights, adopted by the United Nations in 1948, draws on many of the same principles that deists emphasized. The Declaration recognizes the inherent dignity and worth of all human beings and affirms the equal and inalienable rights of all people. These rights include the right to life, liberty, and security of person, as well as the right to freedom of thought, conscience, and religion.

In addition to influencing the development of modern human rights, the deist view of natural rights and equality also contributed to the development of democratic ideals. Deists believed in the power of reason and the importance of individual freedom and choice, which laid the groundwork for modern democratic principles. By rejecting traditional authority and emphasizing individual conscience and natural law, deism helped to establish the idea that governments should be based on the consent of the governed and exist to protect the rights of individuals.

A COMPREHENSIVE LOOK ON DEISM

In summary, the deist movement, with its emphasis on reason, natural law, and individual conscience, played a significant role in the development of the concept of human rights. Deists believed in the inherent rights and equality of all people, which laid the groundwork for modern human rights and democratic principles. The deist rejection of traditional authority and emphasis on individual freedom and choice helped to establish the idea that governments should be based on the consent of the governed and exist to protect the rights of individuals.

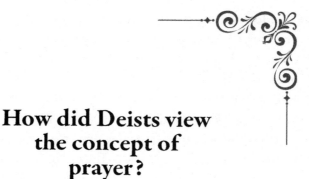

How did Deists view the concept of prayer?

Deists believed in the existence of a God who created the universe and established natural laws but did not intervene in the affairs of human beings. They rejected traditional religious dogma, supernatural events, and organized religions, instead emphasizing the use of reason, observation, and personal experience to understand the world.

Given this perspective, the deist view of prayer was different from that of traditional religious beliefs. Deists rejected the idea that prayer was a means of petitioning God for personal favors or intervention in the world. They believed that God had established natural laws and that these laws could be understood and followed through the use of reason and observation. Therefore, deists did not see prayer as a way to influence God's actions or seek his assistance in human affairs.

However, deists did not reject prayer altogether. They saw prayer as a means of expressing gratitude to God for the natural order and beauty of the universe, as well as a way to reflect on one's own life and actions. For deists, prayer was a personal and introspective act, rather than a way to seek external assistance or intervention from God.

In addition, some deists saw prayer as a way to connect with the divine on a spiritual level. They believed that prayer could be a means of achieving a deeper understanding of the natural world and one's place in it, as well as a way to cultivate personal virtues and moral character. However, even in this sense, prayer was not seen as a way to influence God's actions, but rather as a way to deepen one's own understanding and relationship with the divine.

In summary, the deist view of prayer rejected the traditional idea of petitioning God for personal favors or intervention in the world. Deists believed that God had established natural laws that could be understood and followed through the use of reason and observation. Therefore, prayer was seen as a personal and introspective act, a means of expressing gratitude and reflecting on one's life and actions, as well as a way to connect with the divine on a spiritual level.

What is the relationship between Deism and the concept of personal autonomy?

Deism was a philosophical and religious movement that emerged in the Enlightenment era, which emphasized the use of reason and observation to understand the world and challenged traditional religious authority. Deists believed in the existence of a God who created the universe and established natural laws but did not intervene in the affairs of human beings. They rejected supernatural events, organized religion, and dogmatic beliefs, instead emphasizing individual reason and conscience to interpret religious and moral principles.

Given this perspective, Deism had a significant impact on the development of the concept of personal autonomy. Deists believed that individuals had the freedom to use reason and conscience to interpret religious and moral principles, rather than relying on traditional religious authority. This emphasis on individual autonomy helped to challenge the idea that religious beliefs and practices should be determined by institutions or clergy, rather than by individual conscience.

Furthermore, Deists believed in the inherent dignity and worth of all human beings, which emphasized the importance of individual autonomy. They rejected the idea that some people were born with special privileges or rights, such as those associated with aristocracy or monarchy, and instead argued that all people were entitled to the same rights and protections. This emphasis on individual worth and equality reinforced the importance of personal autonomy in making choices about one's own life and beliefs.

The Deist view of God and the universe also emphasized the natural order and the importance of reason and observation. Deists believed that God had created the universe according to natural laws, which could be discovered through reason and observation. This emphasis on natural law and reason contributed to the development of the concept of personal autonomy. Deists believed that individuals had the capacity to use reason and observation to understand the world and make decisions about their own lives, without the need for external religious or institutional authority.

In addition, the Deist rejection of supernatural events and traditional religious dogma also contributed to the development of the concept of personal autonomy. Deists emphasized the use of reason and personal experience to understand religious and moral principles, rather than relying on supernatural events or religious texts. This emphasis on personal experience and reason helped to challenge the idea that religious beliefs and practices should be determined by external authority, and reinforced the importance of personal autonomy in interpreting and making decisions about religious and moral beliefs.

A COMPREHENSIVE LOOK ON DEISM

In summary, Deism had a significant impact on the development of the concept of personal autonomy. Deists emphasized the use of reason and conscience to interpret religious and moral principles, rejected traditional religious authority, and believed in the inherent dignity and worth of all human beings. Their emphasis on natural law, reason, and personal experience challenged the idea that religious beliefs and practices should be determined by external authority, and reinforced the importance of personal autonomy in making decisions about one's own life and beliefs.

How did Deism influence the development of the concept of religious pluralism?

Deism was a philosophical and religious movement that emerged in the Enlightenment era, which challenged traditional religious beliefs and authority. Deists believed in the existence of a God who created the universe and established natural laws, but did not intervene in the affairs of human beings. They rejected supernatural events, organized religion, and dogmatic beliefs, instead emphasizing individual reason and conscience to interpret religious and moral principles.

Given this perspective, Deism had a significant impact on the development of the concept of religious pluralism. Deists emphasized the importance of individual conscience and the use of reason to interpret religious and moral principles, rather than relying on traditional religious authority. This emphasis on individual interpretation and reason helped to challenge the idea that there was only one true religion or way of interpreting religious beliefs.

Furthermore, Deists believed in the inherent dignity and worth of all human beings, which emphasized the importance of religious pluralism. They rejected the idea that some people were born with special privileges or rights based on their religion, and instead argued that all people were entitled to the same rights and protections regardless of their religious beliefs. This emphasis on individual worth and equality reinforced the importance of religious pluralism in respecting the diversity of religious beliefs.

In addition, the Deist view of God and the universe also contributed to the development of the concept of religious pluralism. Deists believed that God had created the universe according to natural laws, which could be discovered through reason and observation. This emphasis on natural law and reason contributed to the development of the concept of religious pluralism by emphasizing the importance of individual interpretation and the diversity of religious beliefs that could be understood through reason and observation.

Moreover, Deists rejected the idea that one particular religion had a monopoly on truth or salvation. They believed that all religions had some truth to them, and that individuals should be free to interpret religious principles in a way that was consistent with their own conscience and reason. This emphasis on the diversity of religious beliefs and the rejection of religious exclusivity reinforced the importance of religious pluralism as a means of respecting and valuing the diversity of religious beliefs.

A COMPREHENSIVE LOOK ON DEISM

In summary, Deism had a significant impact on the development of the concept of religious pluralism. Deists emphasized the importance of individual conscience and reason in interpreting religious and moral principles, rejected traditional religious authority, and believed in the inherent dignity and worth of all human beings. Their emphasis on natural law, reason, and individual interpretation contributed to the development of the concept of religious pluralism by emphasizing the importance of respecting the diversity of religious beliefs and rejecting the idea of religious exclusivity.

How did Deism view the concept of the universe and its origins?

D eism was a philosophical and religious movement that emerged in the Enlightenment era, which challenged traditional religious beliefs and authority. Deists believed in the existence of a God who created the universe and established natural laws, but did not intervene in the affairs of human beings. They rejected supernatural events, organized religion, and dogmatic beliefs, instead emphasizing individual reason and conscience to interpret religious and moral principles.

The Deist view of the universe and its origins was influenced by the scientific discoveries of the time, which challenged traditional religious beliefs about the nature and origin of the universe. Deists rejected the idea that the universe was created by a supernatural act of God, instead arguing that the universe was created by a rational and intelligent being who established natural laws and then allowed the universe to evolve according to those laws.

Deists believed that the universe was a vast, orderly system that could be understood through reason and observation. They believed that the universe was created by a rational and intelligent being who established natural laws that govern the behavior of all things. This belief in natural law was influenced by the scientific discoveries of the time, which showed that the universe could be explained in terms of natural causes and effects, rather than supernatural intervention.

Furthermore, Deists believed that the universe was a reflection of the rational and intelligent being who created it. They believed that the universe was designed to be understandable to human beings, and that the natural laws that governed the universe could be discovered and understood through reason and observation. This emphasis on reason and observation reflected the scientific approach to understanding the universe that was being developed during the Enlightenment.

Moreover, Deists believed that the universe was created for a purpose, but that purpose was not necessarily known or understood by human beings. They believed that the purpose of the universe was to allow human beings to use reason and observation to understand the natural laws that governed the universe, and to use that understanding to live moral and virtuous lives.

In summary, Deism viewed the universe and its origins as the product of a rational and intelligent being who created the universe and established natural laws, but did not intervene in the affairs of human beings. Deists rejected the idea of supernatural intervention, instead emphasizing the importance of reason and observation in understanding the natural laws that govern the universe. The Deist view of the universe reflected the scientific approach to understanding the natural world that was being developed during the Enlightenment, and emphasized the idea that the universe was designed to be understandable to human beings through reason and observation.

About the Author

Karl S. Moretti is a prominent author who has made significant contributions to the field of religious history, religions, and philosophy. He was born and raised in a small town in Italy, where he developed an interest in theology and philosophy at a young age.

Moretti went on to study theology and philosophy at Rome, where he obtained his bachelor's, master's, and doctoral degrees. During his studies, he became particularly interested in the history of religion and the various ways in which religious beliefs and practices have shaped human societies throughout history.

After completing his education, Moretti began teaching philosophy and religious studies at various universities in Europe and the United States. He quickly gained a reputation as a brilliant scholar and a captivating lecturer, and his classes were always in high demand.

In addition to his teaching, Moretti also began writing extensively on the topics of religious history, religions, and philosophy.

Moretti's work is characterized by its depth and breadth of knowledge, as well as its clear and concise writing style. He has a talent for distilling complex ideas and making them accessible to a wide range of readers, from academics to general readers.

Today, Moretti is widely regarded as one of the leading scholars in his field, and his work continues to shape the way we understand the role of religion in human history and society. His books are considered essential reading for anyone interested in the history of religion, religious studies, or philosophy.

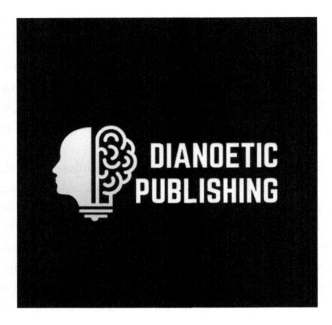

About the Publisher

Welcome to Dianoetic Publishing, the home of thought-provoking and engaging books on a wide range of topics. At Dianoetic, we believe that reading should be a joyful and enriching experience that broadens our minds, challenges our assumptions, and deepens our understanding of the world around us.

Our publishing house is committed to bringing you books that are not only informative and insightful, but also enjoyable to read. We work with some of the most talented and innovative authors from around the world, who are passionate about their subjects and dedicated to making their ideas accessible to a wide range of readers.

At Dianoetic Publishing, you'll find books on everything from history, science, and politics to literature, art, and culture. Our titles cover a diverse range of topics and are suitable for readers of all ages and backgrounds.

Whether you're looking for a fascinating new biography, an inspiring work of fiction, or a thought-provoking exploration of a complex topic, we've got you covered. We believe that reading should be an adventure, and we are excited to take you on that journey with our books.

We are a new and growing publishing house, and we are committed to building a community of readers who share our love of books and our passion for learning. We invite you to join us on this journey and explore the world of ideas with Dianoetic Publishing.

Printed in Great Britain
by Amazon